Big Beans or Little Beans?

and Other Stories for Five-Year-Olds

Other collections by Julia Eccleshare

How Big Jo Tamed the Lion
and Other Stories for Four-Year-Olds

Tobie and the Face Merchant
and Other Stories for Six-Year-Olds

Big Beans or Little Beans?

and Other Stories for Five-Year-Olds

Collected by Julia Eccleshare

Illustrated by Belinda Evans

Collins

Acknowledgements

The publishers are grateful to the following for permission to reproduce copyright material:

Harrap Ltd for *The Jungle House* by Genevieve Murphy from *Reading with Mother* (ed. Fiona Waters); Pelham Books for *Tiger, Brahman and Jackal* from *The Ivory City* by Marcus Crouch; and J. M. Dent & Sons Ltd for Leaf Magic by Margaret Mahy.

William Collins Sons & Co. Ltd
London Glasgow Sydney Auckland
Toronto Johannesburg

This collection first published in Great Britain 1991

Collection copyright © Julia Eccleshare 1991
Illustrations copyright © Belinda Evans 1991

Copyright in the individual stories remains
the property of each author.

ISBN 0 00 183241 7

A CIP record for this book is available
from the British Library

All rights reserved.
No part of this publication may be reproduced,
stored in a retrieval system, or transmitted in any form
or by any means, electronic, mechanical,
photocopying, recording or otherwise, without the prior
permission of William Collins Sons & Co. Ltd,
8 Grafton Street, London Q1X 3LA

Set in Ehrhardt
Printed and bound in Great Britain by
Hartnolls Ltd, Bodmin, Cornwall

Contents

Big Beans or Little Beans? *Saviour Pirotta*	7
Tiger, Brahman and Jackal *Marcus Crouch*	15
The Mouse, the Bird and the Sausage *Brothers Grimm*	22
The Princesses' Tears *Charles Alverson*	27
The Breeze *Robert Leeson*	38
Henry and the Fruit Cake *Angela Bull*	47
The Great Christmas Mix-Up *Elizabeth Laird*	57
A Baby Brother *Not* for Abigail *Mary Hoffman*	65
The Kitten Called Panda *Victoria Whitehead*	73
Thieves in the Garden *Fay Sampson*	81
Pockets *Judith O'Neill*	90

The Jungle House
Genevieve Murphy 105
Leaf Magic
Margaret Mahy 116

Big Beans or Little Beans?

by Saviour Pirotta

Once there was a queen who bought a giant bean.

The queen liked big things. They made her feel rich and powerful. So she gave the bean to her gardener and ordered him to sow it in the most fertile part of her garden.

"I want this bean to grow into the biggest bean tree in the world," insisted the queen.

The gardener, whose name was Jo Lean, wasn't very keen on giant beans. In fact he wasn't very keen on giant anything. "The beans will be too tough to eat," he complained to the queen. "And the tree will use up all the water in my well."

The queen was furious. She started hopping up and down on her throne and gnashing her teeth like most spoilt queens do when they are angry.

"Get out of my palace," she roared at the gardener. "And don't you ever come back again or I'll have you beheaded."

The poor gardener packed his bags and went to live with his mother on a farm. The countryside was very peaceful after the hustle and bustle of the palace. The gardener liked it. He sowed his little beans in his mother's field and waited for them to grow.

The queen sowed her giant bean herself. She grew it in a large china pot which she kept in her courtyard where she could see it every night from her window. And she watered it with a magic potion she had bought from a passing witch at a ridiculous price. The potion was supposed to make the giant bean tree grow even bigger.

As the summer grew old, the eagles that nested in the high mountains of the land could see the farmer growing his beans at one end of the kingdom and the queen growing hers at the other end.

The queen talked to her tree to make it grow larger. But the gardener nipped the buds on his plant to make the beans stay small.

At long last the beans were ready to pick. The gardener's were rather small, but the queen's beans were the biggest anyone had ever seen.

"Hang the beans on the city walls," demanded the queen. "Let my enemies see what a powerful queen I am."

The queen's servants cut down the large pods and carried them to the city walls. It took more than a hundred woodcutters chopping all at once to fell them, and more than a thousand men to carry the beans to the wall. But at last the giant beans were hung where all the world could see them.

Now, across the desert from the queen's

kingdom there lived a prince whose country was as dry as a bone after it has been licked clean. The prince was beside himself with envy when he saw the giant beans.

"It's not fair," he screamed at his vizier. "I want those beans for myself," and he stamped his foot and rattled his crown like most spoilt princes do when they are angry.

The trembling vizier suggested the prince could attack the queen's city and steal the beans. The prince liked the idea. He called for his general and ordered him to prepare the army.

At sunset the prince rode out of his castle on his white horse, while his army marched before him towards the queen's kingdom.

The poor queen didn't know what to do. The soldiers in her army were too fat to fight. All those giant vegetables the queen kept feeding them had made them very flabby indeed.

"My kingdom is in danger," wailed the queen. But there was not much that she

could do.

The prince's army attacked again and again. The queen's army fought back too, but the prince had given each of his soldiers a suit of armour, so the queen's archers could not do much.

At last the queen decided to give up her giant beans. She gathered her people in front of the castle and gave them the bad news. Just then a familiar figure pushed its way through the crowds. It was Jo Lean the gardener.

"Your Majesty," he said, "I think I can help," and he whispered his plan in the queen's ear.

That night Jo Lean slipped out of the city unnoticed. While the prince's soldiers were sleeping, he tiptoed to their camp and scattered his small beans all over the ground.

Then he crept back to the city and waited.

Early the next morning, the prince ordered his soldiers to attack the queen's city again. But . . . what was that terrible noise he could hear? The prince rushed out of his tent. All around him, his soldiers were slipping on the gardener's beans. They sounded like a million tinpot kettles falling to the ground all at once. The din was quite dreadful.

"Get up and fight, you idiots," shouted the prince.

But it was all in vain. No sooner had the soldiers picked themselves up than they would slip on another bean and yet another.

Jo Lean the gardener couldn't stop laughing.

All that dreadful clanging woke up the queen's army. "Hooray," shouted the soldiers as they chased the prince's army away.

The queen was quite relieved. She gave Jo Lean a nice big medal and brought him back as her gardener again. She invited his old mum to come and live in the palace, too.

Jo Lean was very proud.

"I shall grow you anything you want,"

he promised the queen.

"Yes," laughed her royal highness. "But in the future I shall only want normal-sized vegetables. Bigger is not always better, you know."

All the people in the court agreed.

Tiger, Brahman and Jackal

by Marcus Crouch

Hunting through the jungle one day, a tiger got himself caught in a trap. At first he was furious, roaring mightily and lashing the bars with teeth and claws; then, when this did no good, he wept and whined for his lost freedom.

Just then, along came a poor Brahman.

"Holy one," called the tiger. "Please save me, and let me out of this dreadful cage."

"That would never do," said the Brahman. "If I let you out, you will surely eat me up."

"Never!" said Tiger, and he swore a solemn oath. "If you set me free, I will be your servant for ever."

The wretched animal sobbed so miserably that the good Brahman's soft heart was touched, and at last he slipped the catch and opened the cage door.

Out jumped Tiger and grabbed him by the arm. "What a fool you must be to trust a tiger! Now I've got you, do you think I am going to miss my chance of dinner? I'm starving."

Plead as he might, the Brahman could not coax the tiger into sparing him. But the beast's sharp teeth sharpened his wits, and after many arguments he at last got the tiger to agree that they should put his case to three judges.

First the Brahman asked a pipal tree which was shading their path. "It's no use complaining to me," said the tree unsympathetically. "Here I am, giving shelter to anyone who passes by, and all they do in

return is tear off my branches to feed the cattle. Stop snivelling, Brahman, and take your fate like a man!"

That did not cheer the Brahman. Next he turned to a buffalo which was harnessed to a water-wheel. "What a fool you must be," said Buffalo, "if you expect anyone to be grateful! Look at me! When I was a young cow and gave milk, they fed me on good cotton-seed and oil-cake. Now that my udders are dry, all I get is hard labour and short rations."

In despair the Brahman turned to the road and asked for its opinion. "Never expect anything but injustice!" said Road. "Just take my case. I am helpful to everyone. Rich and poor, big and small, they all walk along me and I ease their travel. And what do I get in return? A kick in the face and the hot ashes from their pipes! No," said Road. "Only a fool looks for justice in the world."

As his three judges had all ruled against him, the Brahman turned back sadly to give himself up to the tiger. Just then he came

TIGER, BRAHMAN AND JACKAL

upon a jackal. This one said cheerfully: "Why, whatever's the matter, Holy One? You look as sick as three drowned kittens."

The Brahman told him his story. "I don't understand this," said Jackal. "It seems a mixed-up story. Tell me all over again."

So the Brahman went through the whole thing again. "No, it's no good," said Jackal. "I can't get things sorted out. Let's go back to where it all happened, and then it may be clearer."

So they went back to the cage, where the tiger was standing, growling and sharpening his claws. "You've taken your time," he snarled at the Brahman. "Come along, now. Dinner is served!"

"Yes," thought the poor Brahman. "But only one of us is sitting down to eat it!"

Hoping to live a few minutes longer, he turned pleadingly to the tiger and said: "Just a few words, Mighty One. I must explain something to this jackal who is a bit slow in his wits."

"Very well," growled the tiger. So the

Brahman went slowly through the whole tale again, making it last as long as he could.

"Oh, my poor head!" cried Jackal. "I can't get this sorted out. Start again. Now you, Brahman, were in the cage and Tiger came walking by..."

"No, you fool!" interrupted Tiger. "I was the one in the cage."

The jackal trembled with fright and with the effort of forcing his poor brain into understanding. "Yes, of course," he stammered. "I've got it now. I was in the cage ... that is to say, I wasn't, he was ... oh dear! My weak wits! Let's see. The tiger was in the Brahman, and the cage walked by ... That can't be right. I shall never get it clear. You had better start dinner."

Tiger was maddened by the jackal's stupidity. "I'll make you understand!" he roared in a fury. "Now, see here. I am the tiger."

"Yes, Mighty One."

"And that is the Brahman."

"If you say so, Mighty One."

"And that is the cage."

"I see, Your Excellency."

"Right. Now I was in the cage. Have you got that?"

"Yes ... No ... Not quite. If you please ..."

"What is it?" said Tiger angrily.

"How did you get in?" asked Jackal.

"How did I get in? How do you think I got in, you fool? The usual way."

"Dear oh dear!" said poor Jackal, still confused. "Don't be angry with me, Your Worship. What is the usual way?"

At this Tiger was beside himself with impatience. He jumped up and bounded into the cage, shouting: "This way! Now have you got it into your stupid head?"

"Yes," said Jackal with a grin, and he slammed the door tight. "I quite understand now. And it seems to me that we had better leave things as they are."

The Mouse, the Bird, and the Sausage

by the Brothers Grimm

Once on a time a mouse, a bird, and a sausage became companions, kept house together, lived well and happily with each other, and wonderfully increased their possessions. The bird's work was to fly every day into the forest and bring back wood. The mouse had to carry water, light the fire, and lay the table, but the sausage had to cook.

He who is too well off is always longing for something new. One day, therefore, the

THE MOUSE, THE BIRD AND THE SAUSAGE

bird met another bird, on the way, to whom it related its excellent circumstances and boasted of them. The other bird, however, called it a poor simpleton for its hard work, but said that the two at home had good times. For when the mouse had made her fire and carried her water, she went into her little room to rest until they called her to lay the cloth. The sausage stayed by the pot, saw that the food was cooking well, and, when it was nearly time for dinner, it rolled itself once or twice through the broth or vegetables and then they were buttered, salted, and ready. When the bird came home and laid his burden down, they sat down to dinner, and after they had had their meal, they slept their fill till next morning, and that was a splendid life.

Next day the bird, prompted by the other bird, would go no more into the wood, saying that he had been servant long enough, and had been made a fool of by them, and that they must change about for once, and try to arrange it in another way. And, though the mouse and the sausage also begged most earnestly, the bird would have his way, and said it must be tried. They cast lots about it, and the lot fell on the sausage who was to carry wood, the mouse became cook, and the bird was to fetch water.

What happened? The little sausage went out towards the wood, the little bird lit the fire, the mouse stayed by the pot and waited alone until the little sausage came home and brought wood for the next day. But the little sausage stayed so long on the road that they both feared something was amiss, and the bird flew out a little way in the air to meet it. Not far off, however, it met a dog on the road who had fallen on the poor sausage as lawful booty, and had seized and swallowed it.

The bird sadly took up the wood, flew home, and related what he had seen and heard. They were much troubled, but agreed to do their best and remain together. The bird therefore laid the cloth, and the mouse made ready the food, and wanted to dress it, and to get into the

pot as the sausage used to do, and roll and creep amongst the vegetables to mix them; but before she got into the midst of them she was scalded, and lost her skin and hair and life in the attempt.

When the bird came to carry up the dinner, no cook was there. In its distress the bird threw the wood here and there, called and searched, but no cook was to be found! Owing to his carelessness the wood caught fire, so a conflagration ensued, the bird hastened to fetch water, and then the bucket dropped from his claws into the well, and he fell down with it, and could not recover himself, but had to drown there.

The Princesses' Tears

by Charles Alverson

Once, in a land far away, lived a very poor king. His name was King Otto, and the land in his tiny domain was so barren that it grew only stones, more stones and thorn trees. His peasants were poor, his nobles were poor and even the wild beasts in King Otto's royal forests were poor. It was little wonder that he was known as King Otto the Poor.

But King Otto did have three precious treasures. They were his daughters, the

Princess Ruby, the Princess Sapphire and the Princess Pearl. King Otto loved these daughters well, for they were fair and good and gentle and *never* – well, almost never – complained. But they were precious to him for another reason. And it was for this reason that King Otto kept the princesses hidden high up in the tower of his tumbledown castle.

The three lovely princesses had a secret. Their secret was that whenever they cried, they didn't cry tears. They cried perfectly shaped little gemstones, rubies and sapphires and pearls, worth a great deal of money to their father. It is said that if he could have kept his daughters weeping for eight hours a day, five days a week, he would have been the richest king anywhere. But King Otto would *never* have done that. He loved the princesses too dearly, and was never happier than when he heard their laughter and songs.

However, when the royal coffers were empty, and his lords, knights and peasants were clamouring at the door, King Otto the

THE PRINCESSES' TEARS

Poor would do a very strange thing. First he would climb the ninety-nine steps up to the tower where the princesses lived all alone. This was *very* tiring. "Ninety-seven steps, ninety-eight steps – puff – ninety-nine steps!" he counted. Then King Otto would pound on the big oak door.

"Princess Ruby," he would shout, "are you there?"

"Yes, Father," Princess Ruby would answer.

"Princess Sapphire," King Otto would demand, "are you there?"

"Yes, Father," would say Princess Sapphire.

"Princess Pearl," he would finally shout, "are *you* there?"

"Yes, Father," Princess Pearl would say with a bit of a sigh in her voice, for she knew what was coming.

"Come near the door, daughters," King Otto would command.

"Yes, Father." And the daughters would come near the door.

"Are you listening, daughters?"

"Yes, Father."

"All right, then," King Otto would say, and he would begin to stomp around on the little landing outside the big door making very fierce and ugly expressions and shouting through the door:

"Princess Ruby – I'll – I'll break your doll!"

"Princess Sapphire – I'll – I'll throw your teddy bear out of the window!"

"Princess Pearl – I'll – I'll knock all the stuffing out of your stuffed crocodile!"

King Otto could never have said this to their faces. That's why he shouted it through the door. And though the princesses knew that their father wouldn't *really* be so mean, by this time all three would be crying. And when King Otto opened the door he would find on the stone floor three little piles of precious stones – rubies, sapphires and pearls. He would kiss his daughters, gather up the gems in a leather bag and run back down the ninety-nine steps to his great hall. There he would find jewel merchants

THE PRINCESSES' TEARS

waiting to buy these treasures, and all his subjects waiting to ask King Otto for money.

Then everything was fine for a while until the royal coffers were empty again, and King Otto would have to go through the whole business all over again: ninety-nine steps up, stomp, shout and threaten until he was blue in the face, kiss his tearful daughters, collect the gems and ninety-nine steps down again. This was such hard work that King Otto was losing weight, and some peasants called him King Otto the Skinny, but never to his face.

Things went on this way for some time – which wasn't much fun for anyone – until one day the princesses looked out from their high tower and saw three fine princes riding by on a search for princesses to marry. How very handsome the princes looked, and how much the princesses longed to be rescued!

They all waved their handkerchiefs and shouted: "Oh, help, handsome princes! Come and save us from this tower of

THE PRINCESSES' TEARS

ninety-nine steps!" But the tower was so high that the princes couldn't hear them and kept on riding.

It looked as though they would ride right into the next kingdom, and the princesses were so sad that each cried a single tear which fell – splash! – and turned into a ruby, a sapphire, a pearl. Then, as one, the princesses threw the precious stones down toward the three princes.

Plink! went the ruby on the head of the first handsome prince.

Plonk! went the sapphire on the head of the second handsome prince.

Plunk! went the pearl on the head of the third handsome prince.

"I say," said the handsome princes, "precious gemstones!" And they looked up and saw the three princesses waving from the tower. They all fell in love immediately. Princes and princesses are like that, you know.

The three princes rode immediately to the great gate of King Otto's castle and clamoured to be let in. "Let us in," they demanded, "so that we may rescue those three lovely princesses and carry them off to be our brides."

"No!" said King Otto the Poor.

"Please?" said the princes.

"Would you take away my three precious daughters," asked King Otto, "and deprive me of my only treasures?"

"Yes," said the princes, "we think we would. We *know* we would." For princes do that sort of thing all the time.

"Go away," demanded King Otto, "or I'll turn my peasants, knights and lords on you, and they'll thrash you severely."

"Let us at them, O King Otto the Poor," cried his peasants, knights and lords.

"Yeah, we'll smash them, King Skinny!" cried a very small peasant, but everybody said: "Ssssssshhhhhhh!"

"If we defeat your lords, knights and peasants," asked the princes, "can we claim your lovely daughters as our brides?"

"I suppose so," said King Otto, for he knew the rules.

THE PRINCESSES' TEARS

The three handsome princes rode to the peak of a very steep hill not far from King Otto's ramshackle castle and waited there very bravely while the massed ranks of King Otto's subjects, armed to the teeth, charged up the hill making very fierce noises.

But just as King Otto's peasants were nearly upon them, the first handsome prince threw a handful of copper coins down the hill, and the peasants all chased after them.

And as King Otto's knights were just about upon the princes, the second handsome prince threw a handful of silver coins down the hill, and the knights all chased after them.

Finally, as King Otto's lords were just about upon them, the third handsome prince threw a handful of gold coins down the hill, and the lords all chased after them.

There was nobody left to stop the princes but King Otto – and he was too skinny – so they dashed up the ninety-nine steps into the tower and ran ninety-nine steps down, each with a lovely princess in his arms. They jumped on their fine black chargers and rode swiftly out of King Otto's poor kingdom.

King Otto was left all alone and poorer than ever. And when his lords, knights and peasants had spent all of the princes' coins, they came back to the castle looking *very* sheepish indeed. But they knew it was no good asking King Otto for any more money, so they all went home and went to bed.

A whole year passed, and the royal coffers were so empty that their bottoms shone like mirrors, and King Otto could see his skinny face in them. There wasn't anything left. But then a trumpet sounded, and a herald clad in fine vestments demanded to see King Otto.

"What do *you* want?" asked King Otto crossly. "I haven't any daughters left."

But the herald didn't want a princess. He just asked King Otto to follow him to a far distant kingdom. King Otto didn't have anything else to do, so he followed the

THE PRINCESSES' TEARS

herald until they were approaching three splendid and identical palaces standing side by side by side. And standing in front of each one was one of his daughters with her prince. And in the arms of each princess was a fat little baby.

Each of the three princesses was crying tears of joy to see her old father again. And in front of each was a pile of rubies, sapphires or pearls much larger and finer than any they'd ever cried before. The princes gathered up these gemstones in silken bags and gave them to King Otto.

One of the princes suggested that since King Otto wasn't poor any more they ought to call him King Otto the Good. And they invited him to return once a year to collect the tears of joy wept by his three lovely daughters.

The Breeze

by Robert Leeson

The Breeze was nosing around among the rocks at the foot of the hills. It played lazily with the scent of tiny, newly-opened blue flowers. There was nothing else to do on an early spring morning, and The Breeze was bored.

Suddenly, from above the rocks, came a great rushing sound. The South Wind was
sweeping down the hills. It moved so swiftly
and blew so strongly that the Breeze was jerked up into the cold, clear sky.

THE BREEZE

"Wake up, Dozy!" shouted the South Wind.

"Where are you going?" asked the Breeze.

"Where do you think, Sleepy?"

"I don't know. How could I know?" answered the Breeze.

The South Wind swung round and round in a great circle till the Breeze felt quite dizzy.

"Never, but never, answer a question with a question," puffed the South Wind. "Just listen, Little Breeze, and don't forget. The South Wind blows north, the North Wind blows south, the East Wind blows west, and the West Wind blows east."

"It all sounds crazy to me," said the Breeze, trying hard to stop twisting round and round.

"Not at all. When it warms up, I blow north. When it cools down, the North Wind blows south."

"Supposing you both blow at the same time?"

"Questions, questions! Well, we don't. Because there's only one lot of air and we don't want to fight over it. And, if we did ... well ..."

"Well?" asked the Breeze.

"If we did there wouldn't be a hat left on a head or a leaf left on a tree or a roof left on a house in the whole wide world."

The South Wind stopped whirling.

"I'm off. Can't wait. Long way to go. Got to see how the world's been doing this winter."

"Can I come with you?"

"Of course you can't. It's too far."

"How far?"

"Till I run out of puff, that's how far."

"Can't I come?" pleaded the Breeze. "I've never seen the world."

"Hm," grunted the South Wind. "I can't stop you. Winds blow where they like. And as far as they can. You won't keep up though, you know."

"I will," said the Breeze. "Wait for me, wait ..."

But the South Wind was already on the way

THE BREEZE

up, out and over the little hills and into the great wide plain with its woods and meadows and villages. Trees and houses showed up black against the white snow, but the air was clear and blue and the sun shone. The Breeze flew after the South Wind, following the sound of laughter through the bright sky.

At first the going was good. The Breeze was left far behind, but that didn't matter. It was great just to swoop round through the empty space above the ground.

On and on and on went the Breeze, revelling in the sun's light and warmth, never noticing that the sun had moved across the sky and that it was heading downwards to the west. Little by little the sky grew darker, little by little the air grew colder.

Down below, the open countryside vanished. More and more houses crowded close together, until the ground could no longer be seen, and from the dark streets below came foul smells and clouds of gritty dust.

The Breeze was choked. The Breeze was tired and worn out. As the sun disappeared from sight, the Breeze dropped from the sky into the midst of the grey-brown buildings.

Just as it fell down to the cold, hard street below, a light came on in a house where the window stood open. The Breeze could feel the warmth and was drawn towards it. There, inside the kitchen, a woman was taking off her coat. She stood by the open window and took a deep breath as the Breeze slipped in.

"Oh, it smells like spring," she said. Then she turned and began to put things on to the table. Very soon, the front door of the house burst open and children rushed in, shouting and laughing.

"What a draught!" said the woman. She sounded angry. Putting down the plate of food she had in her hand, she rushed to the window and slammed it. "Come in for your tea," she called.

There was a clatter of shoes on the floor. *Bang* went the front door. *Bang* went

the kitchen door.

The Breeze was shut out in the passage. It was quite dark, and the Breeze was all alone. It rushed up and down the staircase, moaning.

"Just listen to the wind," said one of the children. "You can hear it crying."

"That's not the wind. That's the cat, wanting to come in," answered the mother. "Go and open the back door."

As the back door opened, the Breeze took the chance and blew out again, straight into a small garden. Now it was dark, and there was nothing to be seen. All was still and very cold, freezing cold. The Breeze wandered up and down until the flowers in the garden border told it to go away and let them sleep.

The night was long, and it felt to the Breeze as if it would never end. But at last the light, a cold grey light, came back. White frost stood on the small patch of grass and glistened on the closed buds of the flowers.

From the sky, small snowflakes were swirling. As the Breeze woke up, they

THE BREEZE

whisked round and round, dancing in the air. Then they settled gently on the ground.

From up above there came a whistling, snarling sound. Something was driving the snowflakes through the air, bending the flowers almost down to the earth.

Next moment, the Breeze was caught up and drawn high into the sky. The streets and houses, white with new snow, were left behind and the Breeze heard a sharp, cold voice say:

"Hurry, hurry, hurry!"

"Who's that?" asked the Breeze, as great gusts of air blew this way and that.

"Questions, questions, questions, always questions! I'm the North Wind. Don't hang about like you did yesterday."

"How do you know what I did yesterday?" gasped the Breeze. "I was following the South Wind."

The North Wind laughed with a hard, harsh sound.

"Still half asleep, aren't you? Don't you remember? The North Wind going means the South Wind coming back."

"Will you be the South Wind again, tomorrow?"

"Wait and see, Little Breeze. Wait and see."

Henry and the Fruit Cake

by Angela Bull

This is a story about a dog called Henry, who lived in the days before cars and buses had been invented. There were trains, as you will see, but people travelled along the roads in carts and carriages, pulled by horses. That meant houses needed a stable where horses were kept – and where a naughty dog might be sent until he was good.

Henry was a naughty dog.

When Henry was led, in disgrace, to the

stable, Sophie went too.

"Leave me alone!" growled Henry.

"But I'm sorry for you. Poor Henry! Fancy being spanked, and pushed out of the kitchen," said Sophie.

Sophie was a spaniel. She had a curly coat, floppy ears, and big brown eyes. Her soupy, sympathetic look got on Henry's nerves.

Henry was a mongrel. He had a pointed nose, and a wavy tail, and he was much bigger than Sophie. That was why he needed to eat so much. And he just couldn't say "no" to a fruit cake, left by itself on the kitchen table.

In the stable Henry flopped down on some straw.

"Are you feeling poorly?" Sophie asked kindly.

"No," snapped Henry.

All the same, the fruit cake had been very big. It was nice to lie still, and recover.

One end of the stable was divided into two loose boxes, where the carriage horses lived. The loose boxes were like little rooms, except that there was straw instead of carpet on the floor, and the walls only reached halfway to the ceiling.

The carriage horses raised their long noses, and peered over the walls at Henry and Sophie.

"What are you dogs doing here?" asked one horse, whose name was Bevis.

"I'm looking after Henry," Sophie explained.

"Is he in trouble again?" asked the other horse. Her name was Beauty.

"Well—"

Sophie looked at Henry with her soupy brown eyes.

"Go on. Tell them," growled Henry. He didn't care. He lay with his pointed nose on his paws, wishing his tummy weren't so full.

Sophie bounced up on to the loose boxes, so that she could talk in a whisper. But it was a loud whisper, and Henry could hear perfectly well.

"Little Master Charlie is coming here today, to stay with his grandfather and

HENRY AND THE FRUIT CAKE

grandmother," began Sophie.

"We know *that*," interrupted Beauty.

"We're going to take the carriage to the station, to meet him," said Bevis.

"Oh, I hope I can go too!" yapped Sophie. "But poor Henry may not be taken now."

Even with his eyes shut, Henry guessed that Sophie was giving him her soupy look.

"Anyway," she went on, "the cook made a fruit cake for Master Charlie, and left it on the kitchen table to cool. And Henry sneaked in, and gobbled it all up."

"How greedy!" said Beauty.

"How naughty!" said Bevis.

"He's very sorry," said Sophie.

I'm not, Henry wanted to say. Though he was, a little bit.

"Won't Master Charlie be cross about not having his cake," said Bevis.

"I'm afraid he will," answered Sophie, in the sad, sympathetic voice that got on Henry's nerves.

"I don't suppose," said Beauty, "that Master Charlie will like Henry any more, now that he's eaten the fruit cake."

"I don't suppose he will," sighed Sophie. And that was too much.

"G-rr-rr! Clear off, Sophie!" growled Henry.

He showed his sharp white teeth, and Sophie suddenly remembered it was time for her brushing, and skipped out of the stable.

Henry put his nose down on his paws, and groaned quietly. If he'd known the cake was for Master Charlie, he wouldn't have eaten it. He liked Charlie. It would be terrible if Charlie stopped liking him.

Charlie didn't often visit his grandparents, but when he came, it was fun. He took Henry for runs, and threw sticks and balls for him to fetch. Suppose Charlie was too cross about the cake to play with him?

Henry's nose lay heavily on his paws. He wished he'd never peeped into the kitchen, and seen that silly fruit cake.

Fred, the groom, came into the stable, and began unhooking harnesses from the

HENRY AND THE FRUIT CAKE

wall.

"It's time to go and meet Master Charlie's train," he said to Bevis and Beauty.

There was a slapping of leather, and a clinking of bits and buckles, but through it Henry could still hear the horses talking.

"Won't it be nice to see Master Charlie?" said Bevis.

"Yes. We'll see him. We're not naughty," said Beauty. And her long face rose sneeringly above the wall of the loose box.

Then the horses clattered out into the yard, to be hitched up to the carriage. Henry watched them through the stable door. He saw Charlie's grandparents coming out of the house. Charlie's grandmother had Sophie on a lead. Sophie's curly coat was brushed to a beautiful glossy shine.

"I'm going to the station, Henry," called Sophie. "Isn't that lovely? Oh, sorry!"

"I don't care," growled Henry.

Sophie and the grandparents climbed into the carriage, Fred picked up the reins, and the horses trotted away.

Henry shut his eyes, and fell asleep.

When he woke, he felt better. He pricked up his ears, and looked round the stable. It was time for another meal. He bounced into Beauty's loose box, and sniffed at the manger. Oats and hay! How disgusting! What silly things horses ate.

There was a nice smell of rat, but it was coming from a hole in the wall. Even Henry's sharp nose couldn't poke very far down it.

He sighed, and flopped back on the straw. Then he remembered. Charlie was coming. Sophie and Bevis and Beauty would see him, but Henry wouldn't. He was in disgrace. I shan't let them see that I mind about Charlie, thought Henry. I'll have an adventure, all by myself.

He shut his eyes, and began making plans.

Two arms suddenly clasped themselves round his neck. He felt a kiss on his pointed nose. He looked up, and saw Charlie's smiling face.

For the first time since he ate the fruit cake, his wavy tail began to stir. It wagged and wagged.

"Oh, Henry," said Charlie, "I've been longing to see you! Sophie's all right, but she's rather—"

Soupy, thought Henry.

"They said you were in disgrace," Charlie went on. "You gobbled up a fruit cake that was specially meant for me. Oh, Henry, you *were* clever. Did you remember that I hate fruit cake?"

To be perfectly honest, Henry remarked to himself, I didn't remember. I just saw that big brown cake on the table, and I couldn't resist it.

He licked his lips as he thought of it.

"It was really kind of you," said Charlie. "You're such a nice, naughty, bad, funny, lovely dog! Come on. Let's go for a run!"

The Great Christmas Mix-up

by Elizabeth Laird

One Saturday afternoon, Kevin and his mum went down the High Street to do their Christmas shopping.

Kevin spotted a black leather jacket with studs on.

"Get that for Spike, Mum," he said. "He'd love it."

Mum saw a soft cosy rug.

"Just right for Gran," she said, "when she's sitting watching telly in the evenings."

Kevin found a blue teddy with a ribbon.

It had googly eyes that wobbled when you shook it.

"Katie will like this," said Kevin. "She must be tired of that old fluffy rabbit of hers."

Mum picked out a pair of slippers for Dad.

"Fully lined and going half price," she said. "Much better than those awful old things he wears all the time."

"How about this for Waffles?" said Kevin, holding up a lead. "He's chewed his old one to bits."

"Good idea," said Mum. "Now, Kevin, you look at this nice pile of books for a minute. I've got something to do in the music department."

Kevin smiled to himself. He knew what Mum was up to. She was buying a present for him and she didn't want him to watch. He looked at the books for a moment, but then something shiny on the next stand caught his eye. It was a row of kitchen utensils and right at the front, all bright and sparkling, was a lovely metal egg whisk with a scarlet handle. It was like the one he usually borrowed to make bubbles in the bath, only it was bigger, and brighter, and better.

Quick as a wink, Kevin pulled it off the hook and ran to the woman at the till.

"I want this please," he said in a loud whisper. "It's for my mum."

The woman smiled at him.

"Have you got any money?" she said.

Kevin pulled some money out of his pocket. He'd been saving up for weeks to do his Christmas shopping. The lady picked out two pound coins and one fifty pence coin and wrapped the egg whisk in a paper bag.

"There you are, dear," she said. "Be careful, mind, and don't get your fingers caught in it."

On Christmas Eve, Kevin and Mum wrapped up all their Christmas presents and put them under the Christmas tree. The pile looked beautiful; all mysterious,

THE GREAT CHRISTMAS MIX-UP

and crackly, and exciting. They were just standing back to admire the effect when the door burst open. In came Spike and Waffles.

Suddenly, everything happened at once. Waffles saw the parcels and made a dash at them. He started chewing the paper off. Spike let out a howl and made a dash at Waffles. He knocked the Christmas tree over. Mum shrieked and grabbed the Christmas tree. She just managed to catch it in time. Kevin nearly burst into tears.

"It's all right," said Spike, when he'd got hold of Waffles. "Just you leave it to me. You two take Waffles off into the kitchen, and I'll clear it all up."

When Kevin went back into the sitting room, Spike had nearly finished. He was looking very pleased with himself.

"Looks smashing, doesn't it?" he said to Kevin.

Kevin nodded. Spike was right. It did look very nice, but somehow things weren't quite the same. There was something about the Christmas tree . . . and then some of

the parcels seemed to have changed their shape...

On Christmas morning, the great moment came. Everyone gave presents to everyone else. Kevin got some Lego, and a suit of armour, and a book, and a puzzle, and a beautiful garage with cars that fitted neatly inside it. Spike got a set of new mirrors for his motorbike, Gran got a book of knitting patterns, Mum got a box of her favourite chocolates, and Dad got some funny socks.

"Here," said Spike, when the floor was already deep in wrapping paper. "We forgot these ones under the tree. Look, Gran, here's one for you."

Gran quickly ripped off the paper, and pulled her present out.

"Oh!" she said. "A leather jacket! With studs on! Just what I've always wanted. It'll keep the wind off me when I'm fishing."

Spike got his next.

"Hey!" he said. "What a nice little ted! Real cool eyes. It'll be my mascot. Thanks, Mum."

Then it was Dad's turn.

"A rug!" he said, when he'd opened his present. "Just what I need when I'm out bird-watching. I nearly froze to death last week."

Katie had been trying to open her parcel for ages. She couldn't get the paper off. Gran had to help her.

"Nice string! Nice string!" she said, when she got the dog's lead out at last. She was so happy, she dribbled. She carefully looped it round the funnel of her train, and started pulling it round the room.

"Choo! Choo! Choo!" she said.

Waffles had helped himself to his present. Dad was the first to notice him.

"Here, that's a good idea," he said, "giving Waffles a pair of slippers of his own. Now perhaps he'll leave my nice old ones alone."

Mum and Kevin looked at each other and laughed.

"I think we'd better open ours now, don't you?" she said. She got the paper off first. Inside was a cassette of pop music.

"It's a good thing we both like the same groups, isn't it, Kevin?" she said. "This'll keep me company when I'm washing the car."

Kevin was too happy to answer her. He was looking at the whisk, his whisk. He'd play with it in the bath that very night. It would make the biggest, the best, the most beautiful bubbles he had ever seen. And it was his very own.

A Baby Brother *Not* for Abigail

by Mary Hoffman

Nobody asked Abigail if she wanted a baby brother, but she got one anyway. When her mother grew a bump in front of her that took up the place where her lap used to be, she told Abigail that it was going to be a new baby.

"What's wrong with your old baby?" asked Abigail, trying to fit on what was left of the lap, but her mother just laughed.

After that, people started asking if she wanted a baby brother – *or* a baby sister!

"Neither," said Abigail, but Dad said that was rude and besides, it would upset Mum. After that, when people asked the question, Abigail just said "Would you like to see my Lego dungeon?" or anything to get them talking about something else.

Actually, when baby Max *did* come, it wasn't too bad. For a start, Abigail went to stay with her granny, who made toffee and all sorts of things that weren't allowed at home and who bought her a pair of roller boots. Then, when Dad took her into the hospital, it was nice to see Mum almost her proper shape again. The baby looked quite sweet too, if you liked that sort of thing.

The best part was going into school on Monday and telling everyone about it during Show and Tell. No one had ever been very interested in Abigail's Shows or Tells, which were mainly about caterpillars and things like that. But everyone seemed to think a new baby brother was much better than a furry ginger caterpillar. And the day that Mum first brought Max to collect her in his pram . . . well! Abigail had never been so popular.

She was popular at home, too, for a while. Lots of visitors came to the house to see Max and give him presents and most of them brought something for Abigail too. "We don't want her to feel left out, do we?" they whispered.

But after about two weeks, Abigail was totally fed up with the baby. He couldn't *do* anything and what was worse, Mum didn't seem to be able to do anything either. She looked after Abigail, of course, made her dinners and brought her clean socks in the morning and took her to school, but she didn't play with her any more or read to her or have interesting chats. She chatted to Max instead and tickled his toes and blew raspberries in his fat neck.

Abigail began to understand what the visitors had meant about feeling left out. Not that she wanted her toes tickled, of course, but she wouldn't have minded a bit of help with her marble run. She decided to talk to Scott about it. Scott was her friend at school and he had *two* baby brothers. Well, one was a baby, born a week or two before Max, and the other was nearly three, more like a person.

"Don't you mind your mum having more babies?" Abigail asked Scott at their next playtime.

"Not really," he said. "I minded about Robert but it doesn't seem to matter so much about Christopher."

"What did you mind about Robert?" asked Abigail, really interested.

"Oh, you know, all that crying and being smelly and everyone saying how sweet he was."

"But he's not smelly now and he doesn't cry much at all," said Abigail.

"No, he's OK now," said Scott. "You can play marbles with him. I suppose that's why I don't mind so much about Christopher. I know he'll be all right when he's stopped being a baby."

"Don't you like babies, then?" asked Abigail.

"They're all right," said Scott cautiously. "I mean, they're all little and quite funny really. But I wouldn't want to *be* one. I'm glad I'm the eldest."

Abigail thought about this a lot for the rest of the day and took a new look at Max when she next saw him. He *was* very little and he *did* pull some funny faces.

"I'm glad I'm not a baby," she told her mother.

"So am I," said her mother. "I couldn't cope with two at once." She gave a big yawn.

Abigail was surprised. "Don't you like babies, Mum?" she asked.

"Oh yes, they're very sweet and little and funny, but they are such hard work and they make you so tired," said Mum, yawning again.

"Then why did you have another one?" Abigail almost shouted.

"Because when they stop being little and funny they can talk and play and do interesting things like you. They don't stay babies for ever, you know."

Abigail was beginning to see that this was true. Max was already looking differ-

ent.

"When do you think he'll be able to play marbles?" she asked.

Her mother laughed. "I think you'll have to wait a while for that. But I tell you what. When I've given him his next feed and put him down for a rest, *I'll* give you a game."

This was the best offer Abigail had had since Max was born. She waited patiently while Max was fed, slurping greedily and noisily from their mother's breasts. Then she came and watched while his nappy was being changed.

"Yuck," she said. "How can you bear to?"

"It's all part of looking after him," said her mother. "He can't change his own, after all, can he? And I did all the same things for you, when you were a baby."

Abigail had never thought of that. "Yes, and I turned out all right, didn't I?"

Her mother laughed. "Yes, you did, and I'm sure Max will too. But we can't wait till he's four before we love him, so I'm making a start now, just as I did with you."

Abigail thought about herself as a baby and she was glad her mother had loved her even then. Then she thought about what it would have been like to have a big sister who didn't want her.

"I'm glad I'm the eldest," she said, as her mother put Max down in his crib. "And I'm going to try not to wait until he's four before I like him."

"Fair enough," said Mum. "After all, Dad and I had him because we wanted another child for us not just a brother for you. Now, how about those marbles?"

And Abigail ran off to get them.

The Kitten Called Panda

by Victoria Whitehead

Mark and Jenny had always wanted a kitten, and now they had seen just the one they wanted. It was for sale in the window of a shop. The shop belonged to Mr Wand.

"Look at that kitten, Dad! Isn't it sweet?" cried Jenny, as she and Mark and Dad passed the shop.

"It's black and white," said Mark excitedly. "It's got patches over both eyes – it looks just like a panda!"

"Please, Dad," begged both children

THE KITTEN CALLED PANDA

together. "Can we have it? We can call it Panda!"

Dad was not sure whether or not he wanted to buy anything, let alone a kitten, from Mr Wand's shop. It was not a pet shop, even though it sold kittens. It was not a grocer's shop, even though it sold food. It was not a chemist, even though it sold strange potions, and it was not a toy shop even though it sold boxes of magic tricks. It looked like a magic shop to Dad, and he was not sure about it at all. But the children shouted and jumped up and down and tugged on his sleeve, so much and so noisily that, in the end, he agreed to go inside.

Mr Wand smiled when he heard that the children wanted the kitten and that they had already thought up a name. He took a bottle of magic potion down from a very high shelf. The words written on the bottle were PANDA POTION.

"If you're going to call the kitten Panda," said Mr Wand, "you'll be needing a bottle of this. Just give him a spoonful a day and come back to me as soon as it's finished."

Dad looked at the potion and the children looked at Dad.

"Can we have the kitten? *Please*, Dad," they said.

Dad looked at Mr Wand and then he looked at the kitten.

"*Please*, Dad," they said again.

At last Dad agreed.

"That will be fifty pence exactly," said Mr Wand, as he put the kitten and the potion into a basket for the children to take away. "And I think you'll find that that's the best fifty pence worth you ever had in your life."

At first Panda slept in a shoebox in Mark and Jenny's kitchen. He drank milk out of a saucer into which Mark and Jenny put one spoonful of the magic potion every day.

He grew very fast. His ears grew round instead of pointed, and his long tail became a short one. Soon he had to sleep in a grocery box from the supermarket, and drink milk from a soup bowl. And still he was

THE KITTEN CALLED PANDA

having one spoonful of magic potion a day. He grew fat and soft and furry and very big indeed.

Panda did not grow into a cat like the cats that belonged to the other children who lived in Mark and Jenny's road. For one thing, he grew so big that he could no longer sleep in the grocery box. Instead he had to sleep sprawled out in Dad's favourite television chair, and he still spilt over the edge. For another thing, he drank so much milk that in the end the children got tired of filling and refilling his soup bowl and decided to feed him from a great big bucket. And, for a third thing, Panda absolutely refused to eat cat food.

When Panda had finished the whole bottle of Panda Potion and gallons and gallons and gallons of milk, Dad, Jenny and Mark went back to have a serious talk with Mr Wand.

"Panda's grown much too big," Dad grumbled, "and he spends all day and all night in my favourite television chair."

"And he only drinks milk," said Jenny.

THE KITTEN CALLED PANDA

"Out of a bucket."

"And we don't know what to give him to eat," Mark added ruefully. "He doesn't like cat food."

"I should try him on this, then," smiled Mr Wand, handing them three heavy sacks and another bottle of Panda Potion.

"What on earth is it?" Dad asked, pulling a long stick out from the sack. The stick had green pointed leaves.

"Well, if you've got a panda for a pet," said Mr Wand, "then it stands to reason that you are going to need some bamboo to feed him."

Soon Panda grew big enough to cuddle the children on his knee. He spent hours playing in the fruit trees, and especially loved the garden swing, which was made out of a big black tyre and two ropes. Dad had to sit on the sofa to watch television because his chair was always occupied by the panda.

One day, Jenny and Mark and Dad were walking past Mr Wand's shop again. There were some more kittens in the window.

"Aren't they sweet?" cried Jenny excitedly. "We *love* Panda, but can't we have a kitten as well?"

"That little one's got black and yellow stripes!" Mark cried, "and a long stripy tail. It looks just like a tiger. Can we have it?"

But Dad was already peering anxiously into Mr Wand's shop. He could see Mr Wand smiling to himself as he stood behind the counter, waiting for them to come in. He had a bottle in his hand. On it were written the words TIGER TONIC.

"Please, Dad, can we have the kitten? We can call it Tiger!" the children shouted.

Now, much as Dad loved Panda, he did not really want to have a kitten in the house that might grow up to be a tiger. After all, where would a tiger sleep at night? What would a tiger need to play with? And whatever would they give a tiger to eat?

"*Please*, Dad, can we?" said the children, jumping up and down and tugging on his sleeve. But Dad shook his head, slowly at first, then faster, then very fast indeed.

He guided the children hurriedly away from Mr Wand's magic shop.

"If you like, we *will* get another kitten," he said. "But I don't think we should get it from here."

"Oh," sighed Mark, disappointed. "All right."

"And what's more," Dad continued, "you have to promise me something first."

"Yes," said Jenny quickly, "anything you like."

"Promise me," said Dad, "that you won't call the kitten Panther or Tiger or Elephant or any name like that. One wild animal in the house is quite enough."

"We promise," said the children.

And they kept their promise, too. When Dad came home next day with a beautiful little ginger kitten for them, they decided, just to be on the safe side, to call it Cat.

Thieves in the Garden

by Fay Sampson

Elaine had made her own bird table.

It was a big post with a flat board on top. There was a hook in the side to hang a bag of nuts on. It had been quite hard to hammer the nails in. Mum had had to help her a bit.

Her sister Janet and her brother Tom were making bird tables too. They were showing off, as usual. Their tables had little roofs over them.

"Choose a good place to put them,"

Mum had said. "Somewhere where the cats won't be able to jump up on them."

Tom set his up by the goldfish pond. Janet put hers nearer the garden shed.

"I'm going to put mine in front of the window," said Elaine. "Then I can watch the birds having their food while I have mine."

Mum gave them some bread and bacon fat, and a bag of nuts for each of them. Elaine had to stand on a chair to put the food on hers.

"Come indoors and watch what happens," said Mum.

It was a cold day. There were not many birds about. Elaine watched and waited until it began to get dark.

"Never mind," said Dad, when he came home to tea. "You'll have fun watching them at breakfast-time."

As soon as she got up next morning, Elaine ran into the kitchen. She climbed up on a stool and looked out of the window. Her bird table was empty. All the food had gone. Even the bag of nuts.

"You put it too near the house. The cat must have got it," said Janet. "Mine's better." But when she looked, hers was empty too. So was Tom's.

"That's funny," said Mum. "I shouldn't have thought a cat could have climbed up the post and got on to the table."

They put more food out, and a dish of warm water because it was a frosty morning. A few birds flew down. They quickly ate a good breakfast.

"House sparrows," said Tom, who always liked to know everything.

"I *know*," said Elaine.

By bedtime there was still plenty of bird-food left. But in the morning it had all gone.

"Could it be an owl?" asked Janet. "Stealing it in the night?"

"Owls don't eat nuts," scoffed Tom.

"How do you know?" asked Elaine. "You don't know everything."

"They just don't."

They left another lot of scraps on their tables. It snowed a bit in the night. All the

THIEVES IN THE GARDEN

food had disappeared again in the morning.

"It's not a cat," Janet said, running in from the garden. "There aren't any paw-marks in the snow. Just some funny sort of scratches on the top of the table."

"Let's get up early tomorrow," Dad said. "We'll keep very quiet and watch."

When they woke up, nobody went down to the kitchen. They all waited, not making a sound, at Elaine's bedroom window, which looked down at the back garden.

Then Janet pointed. The tree on the other side of the wall was swaying. A branch swung up and down as something leapt on to the roof of the shed. It was thin and grey, with little pointed ears and a tail like a bush. It jumped on to Janet's table and scoffed all the crumbs. There was a shaking in the bushes. Another one leapt on to Tom's table and gobbled the food. A third one came bounding along the top of the garden fence. It sailed through the air and landed on Elaine's table. It bit open the bag of nuts and began stuffing them into its mouth as fast as it could.

"Grey squirrels!" said Tom. "Of course!"

"The rotten thieves! They're stealing all our poor birds' food." Janet was quite red and cross.

"It's costing me a fortune in nuts," said Mum.

"Tell you what," said Dad. "Let's have a challenge. See who can think up the best idea for stopping the squirrels."

All through breakfast the children were very quiet. They were each trying to think of a brilliant plan.

Tom went out into the garden and started pacing up and down. He seemed to be measuring the lawn. Then he pulled the post of his bird table out of the ground and hammered it into the very middle of the grass.

"I'd like to see them jump *that* far," he grinned.

Janet was busy in the shed. She came out and fixed a net all round her table.

"The squirrels will get caught in it, but the birds will be able to fly in over

the top."

She looked very pleased with herself.

"What are you going to do, Elaine?" asked Mum.

Elaine shook her head. She couldn't think of anything. She couldn't put hers in the middle of the lawn now, because Tom's was there. And she certainly wan't going to do the same as Janet. She wanted to think of a really special idea, but it wouldn't come.

"Elaine's a baby," said Tom. "Let's leave her out."

Then Elaine turned round. She was smiling. She went up to Dad and whispered in his ear.

"Are you sure that's what you want to do?" asked Dad doubtfully.

"Yes," she said.

He got a big piece of card.

"Right. What does it have to say?"

"Keep off, squirrels."

Tom hooted with laughter. "You're joking! Squirrels can't read."

"How do you know?" shouted Elaine.

THIEVES IN THE GARDEN

"Oh, let her do it if she likes," said Janet. "She won't win, will she?"

Dad helped Elaine write the words.

KEEP OFF,
SQUIRRELS!

She liked the shapes of the letters, and the look of the sign in Dad's writing. She nailed it on her table, and it flapped in the wind.

The children went off to school. When they came home, some more birds had been at their table. But there was still lots of food left.

"We'll see what happens in the morning!" said Janet. "I'm sure to win."

"Rubbish!" said Tom. "Mine's as safe as houses."

Elaine didn't say anything.

They woke up next morning and raced into the garden. Janet ran to the shed and stopped in dismay. Her bird table was empty. Tom could see from the back door that his food was all gone. They all turned to look at Elaine's. She hadn't a chance with her silly notice, had she?

Tom's mouth fell open.

Two bluetits were pecking the fat Elaine had left for them. A robin flew down and snatched a crumb of bread. There was plenty of food for all the birds who wanted it.

"But that's ridiculous!" said Janet. "Squirrels can't read!"

"You see?" Elaine smiled. "You don't know everything!"

Pockets

by Judith O'Neill

Brrrr! Brrrr! Brrrr!

Meron's grandma was sewing again. Grandma loved sewing. She made yellow curtains and red cushions to brighten up her house. She made flowery dresses for herself and stripy green pyjamas for Grandpa. She made blouses and shirts and trousers and skirts for her fifteen grandchildren. But best of all, she loved making new clothes for Meron. Meron was her youngest grandchild. Meron was almost six.

Brrrr! Brrrr! Brrrr!

Grandma's sewing-machine was very old. She'd had it for fifty years. It wasn't an electric sewing-machine and it didn't have a treadle to work with her feet. It had a little wheel on one side. Grandma turned the wheel with a handle. The wheel spun round very fast and the needle flew up and down.

Brrrr! Brrrr! Brrrr!

Whenever Meron heard that sound, she hoped Grandma would be making something for her. "What are you making, Grandma?" Meron would say, climbing up high to get a better look at the sewing and trying to guess what it could be.

Grandma would smile at her and say, "Just you wait and see! It won't be very long. I've almost finished." And sometimes she would add, "Then you can try it on."

Meron didn't like waiting. "Is it a dress, Grandma? Is it a shirt?"

"Just you wait and see!" Grandma would say with a mysterious smile.

POCKETS

One day, Meron came to visit Grandma all by herself. It wasn't very far. The front door was open. Meron walked straight into the house.

Brrrr! Brrrr! Brrrr!

Grandma was sewing again! Meron ran to the kitchen. Grandma was turning the handle on her machine very fast. The little wheel spun round and round. The needle flew up and down.

"What are you making, Grandma? Is it something for me?"

Grandma smiled. "Just you wait and see! It won't be very long. I've almost finished. Then you can try it on."

Meron climbed up on to a chair. She stared at the sewing as it ran under the needle, but she couldn't tell what Grandma was making. It was something blue. Bright, bright blue. It looked a bit like a dress but it wasn't quite a dress. It looked a bit like a shirt but it wasn't quite a shirt. It looked a bit like a coat but it wasn't quite a coat.

"What can it be?" asked Meron.

"Just you wait and see!" said Grandma

with a mysterious smile.

Brrrr! Brrrr! Brrrr!

"There we are!" said Grandma, at last. "Now you can try it on." She held it up in her hands for Meron to see.

"What is it?" asked Meron. "Is it a new kind of dress?"

"No, it isn't a dress," said Grandma.

"Is it a new kind of shirt?"

"No, it isn't a shirt."

"Then it must be a coat. A funny sort of coat."

"No, it isn't a coat. Now put up your arms and I'll slip it right over your head."

"On top of my dress?" asked Meron.

"Yes, on top of your dress," said Grandma.

Meron held up her arms. Grandma pulled the wide head-hole right over Meron's head. She pushed one arm gently into one long sleeve. She pushed the other arm gently into the other long sleeve. There was elastic round the wrists.

Meron looked down. The new blue coat that wasn't really a coat hung right

to the bottom of her dress. "There aren't any buttons," said Meron, "so it can't be a coat."

"No, it isn't a coat. Now, I'll tell you what it is. It's a smock!" said Grandma with a big proud smile.

"Whatever is a smock?" asked Meron.

"A smock is a very useful thing. When I was a little girl like you, I wore a smock every day. You put it on over your dress or over your jeans. It keeps you nice and clean. You can spill paint on your smock and no one will mind. You can tear holes in your smock and no one will care. You can crawl under the house or dig in the garden or climb up the tree in your smock and no one will tell you to stop. The smock will get dirty but your clothes will stay clean."

"So it's a bit like an apron?" said Meron.

"A bit like an apron. But it's got long sleeves. And it doesn't have strings to tie at the back. So it's not quite an apron. You just slip it on over your head."

"I think I'm a bit too old for a smock, Grandma," said Meron. "I'm nearly six, you know!"

"No, you're not too old. Not too old at all. Grown-up people wear smocks. Artists wear smocks when they paint. To keep themselves clean."

"I see," said Meron. "I'm quite a good artist myself."

"You are," said Grandma. "So I made you a smock. And I made lots of pockets. I know you like pockets. I put four on the front and two at the back."

Meron did like pockets. She tried out all the pockets on her new blue smock. Two at the top and two at the bottom and two right round at the back. Meron put her hand down into every single pocket. She had to stretch first her right arm and then her left arm to reach all the way round to the back. They were very big pockets. There was plenty of room for her hand.

"I do like the pockets," said Meron. "I could put things inside them."

"That's just what I thought," said Grandma.

Meron looked round the kitchen. She

looked up high at the shelves. She looked down low at the floor. "What could I put in my pockets?" she asked.

"I could give you a bun," said Grandma.

"Thank you," said Meron. "In case I get hungry."

Meron put the bun in a pocket at the bottom. "What else could I put in my pockets?" she asked.

"I could give you a knife. A tiny little knife. It's called a pocket-knife. So it's just the very thing for the pocket in your smock."

"Thank you," said Meron. "In case I want to cut something."

Meron put the knife into a top pocket. "What else could I put in my pockets?" she asked.

"I could give you a pencil and a nice piece of paper."

"Thank you," said Meron. "In case I want to draw something."

Meron folded the paper. She put the pencil and the paper into a pocket right round at the back. She had to stretch.

POCKETS

"What else could I put in my pockets?" she asked.

"I could give you a button. A little white button and a needle and some thread."

"Thank you," said Meron. "In case I want to sew something."

Meron put the button and the needle and the thread into a bottom pocket. "What else could I put in my pockets?" she asked.

"I could give you a map. It's not very big. It's a map of our town."

"Thank you," said Meron. "In case I get lost."

Meron put the map into a pocket right round at the back. She had to stretch. "I've still got one empty pocket. What else could I have?"

Grandma thought very hard. "I could give you some seeds. A packet of seeds. They're tiny sunflower seeds."

"Thank you," said Meron. "In case I want a garden."

Meron put the seeds in to the last pocket at the top of her smock.

"Now I'm ready for anything. I think

I'll go out."

"Don't go too far, Meron. You must stay in our street."

Meron walked out through Grandma's front door. She walked out through the gate. She walked along the footpath. She didn't go far.

"Oh dear, oh dear!" said a lady on the footpath. A thin, thin lady with rather rumpled hair.

"Whatever's the matter?" said Meron with a smile.

"I'm afraid I've lost my way. I was looking for Nettle Street but this seems to be Violet Street."

"I could lend you a map. A map of our town. It's just here in my pocket in my new blue smock." Meron put her hand down into a pocket right round at the back. She had to stretch. She pulled out the map.

"Oh, thank you," said the lady. She looked at the map. "Now I see where I am. Nettle Street's not far. It's only round the corner. I'm so glad I met you! What a wonderful smock!" And the thin, thin lady walked off.

"Oh dear, oh dear!" said a big girl on the footpath. A great big girl with a ribbon in her hair.

"Whatever's the matter?" said Meron with a smile.

"I'm terribly hungry. I forgot to eat my breakfast. I was in such a hurry to go out for a swim."

"I could give you a bun. Do you think that would help you? It's just here in my pocket in my new blue smock." Meron put her hand into a bottom pocket and she pulled out the bun.

"Thank you," said the girl and she ate the bun quickly. "Now I don't feel hungry. I'm so glad I met you. What a wonderful smock!" And the great big girl ran off.

"Oh dear, oh dear!" said a schoolboy on the footpath. A friendly freckled schoolboy in a nice new shirt.

"Whatever's the matter?" said Meron with a smile.

"I've lost a white button. A little white

button. From the front of my shirt."

"I could give you a button. A little white button. And a needle and some thread. They're just here in my pocket in my new blue smock." Meron put her hand down into a bottom pocket. She pulled out the button. She pulled out the needle and the thread.

"It's just the right size!" said the schoolboy on the footpath. "It won't take a minute. I can easily sew it on."

Meron watched the boy. He sewed it very well. Soon the button was on.

"Thank you," said the schoolboy. "That's just what I needed. Here's your needle back again. I'm so glad I met you. What a wonderful smock!" And the friendly freckled schoolboy skipped off.

"Oh dear, oh dear!" said an old man on the footpath. A sprightly old man with a neat white beard.

"Whatever's the matter?" said Meron with a smile.

"I thought I had some seeds. Some seeds for my garden. But now I've gone

POCKETS

and lost them. I don't know what to do!"

"I could give you some seeds. They're tiny sunflower seeds. They're just here in my pocket in my new blue smock." Meron put her hand into a top pocket. She pulled out the packet of tiny sunflower seeds.

"Oh thank you!" said the man. "I'll plant them in my garden. I'm so glad I met you. What a wonderful smock!" And the sprightly old man hurried off.

"Woof-woof, woof-woof!" barked a white dog on the footpath. A small white dog with a long hairy coat.

"Whatever's the matter?" said Meron with a smile.

"Woof," said the dog and he stretched up his head.

"You've got string round your neck! It's tied far too tightly! Now what could I do? I could lend you my knife. It's a tiny pocket-knife. It's just here in my pocket in my new blue smock." Meron put her hand into her top pocket. She pulled out the knife. "Shall I cut it for you? You couldn't hold a knife."

"Woof!" said the dog.

"Just keep quite still," said Meron. "It really won't hurt you." She cut the string.

"Woof-woof!" said the dog as he moved his head quickly, and he bounded off.

Meron put the knife back into her top pocket.

"Oh dear, oh dear!" sighed a very tall policeman. A tired, worried policeman with a hot red face.

"Whatever's the matter?" said Meron with a smile.

"I thought I had some paper. Some paper and a pencil. But I think I must have lost them. And I have to write a note."

"I could give you some paper. I could lend you my pencil. They're just here in my pocket in my new blue smock." Meron put her hand into her very last pocket. A pocket right round at the back. Of course, she had to stretch. She took out the paper and she took out the pencil.

"Oh thank you! Yes, thank you!" said the very tall policeman. He wrote a little note. He put it in his pocket and he gave her back the pencil. "I'm so glad I met you. What a wonderful smock!" And the very tall policeman strode off.

Meron walked back along the footpath. She came to Grandma's gate. The front door was open. She walked straight into the house.

Brrrr! Brrrr! Brrrr!

Grandma was sewing again. Meron ran into the kitchen. Grandma was turning the handle on her machine very fast. The little wheel spun round and round. The needle flew up and down.

"What are you making, Grandma? Is it something for me?"

"Just you wait and see. It won't be very long. I've almost finished. Then you can try it on."

And Grandma smiled her mysterious smile.

The Jungle House

by Genevieve Murphy

John never quite knew how he got there. All he could remember was standing in front of a yellow door and looking up at the sign which said "The Jungle House" in very large letters. He looked everywhere for a bell to ring or a knocker to knock, but he couldn't find one. "It seems a bit rude just to walk in," he thought, "but there's nothing else I can do." So he turned the handle and walked in through the front door.

THE JUNGLE HOUSE

The hall was enormous and, to John's great surprise, it was full of brightly coloured birds. They were perched on the banisters, swinging on the light, flying round the room and hopping across the floor. In the middle of the room, standing on a big table, there was a large parrot.

"Hello," said the parrot.

"Hello," said John, looking round the hall in amazement. "I never expected to see birds in a house. Shouldn't you be in a cage?"

"No *thank you*," said the parrot. "How would you like to spend your life in a cage?" And John had to admit that he wouldn't like it at all. He wondered whether he could persuade his mother to let him have birds flying all round the house, but somehow he didn't think so.

Then John decided he would like to explore. So he said goodbye to the birds and walked through a door into the sitting room.

Stretched out on a rug in front of the fire, he found an enormous lion.

"What an extraordinary place to find a lion," said John.

"What's so extraordinary about it?" asked the lion.

"Nothing, I suppose," said John, "but what happens if someone wants to sit by the fire?"

"Don't be silly," answered the lion, "animals have fur coats to keep them warm. They don't need to sit by a fire."

When he had finished speaking, the lion gave a huge yawn and, before John could answer, he was fast asleep.

So John tiptoed out of the sitting room and said hello to the birds again. "I think you ought to be a bit quieter," he said. "The lion has just gone to sleep." But the birds went on singing as loudly as ever.

So John went on to the dining room. Lying across the table, he found the most enormous elephant.

"What an extraordinary place to find an elephant," said John.

"What's so extraordinary about it?" asked the elephant.

THE JUNGLE HOUSE

"Nothing, I suppose," said John, "but what happens if everyone wants to sit down for a meal?"

"Don't be silly," answered the elephant, "no one wants to eat in a dining room. It's much more fun to have a picnic in the garden."

When he had finished speaking, the elephant gave a huge yawn and, before John could answer, he was fast asleep.

So John tiptoed out of the dining room and said to the birds, "Please do be a little quieter. The elephant's asleep now as well." But the birds went on singing loudly.

So John went on to the kitchen. Curled up on the draining board, he found an enormous brown bear.

"What an extraordinary place to find a bear," said John.

"What's so extraordinary about it?" asked the bear.

"Nothing, I suppose," said John, "but what happens when somebody wants to wash up the cups and saucers?"

"Don't be silly," answered the brown

bear, "animals never bother with cups and saucers. We don't have any washing up."

When he had finished speaking, the brown bear gave a huge yawn and, before John could answer, he was fast asleep.

So John tiptoed out of the kitchen and said to the birds, "Really, I do think you should be a bit more considerate. The lion is asleep, and the elephant, and the brown bear."

"They're used to the singing," said the parrot. "If all the birds were quiet, the animals would be woken up by the silence."

"I've never heard of that before," said John doubtfully. He was about to explain that his mother and father could sleep through any amount of silence, but then he realised that the parrot was fast asleep as well.

So John went upstairs to the bathroom. Sitting up in the bath, he found an enormous giraffe.

"What an extraordinary place to find a giraffe," said John.

THE JUNGLE HOUSE

"What's so extraordinary about it?" asked the giraffe.

"Nothing, I suppose," said John, "but what happens when somebody wants a bath?"

"Don't be silly," answered the giraffe. "No one wants to bath in a bathroom. It's more fun to swim in the lake."

When he had finished speaking, the giraffe gave a huge yawn and, before John could answer, he was fast asleep.

So John tiptoed out of the bathroom and peeped over the banisters. It seemed much quieter now, because some of the other birds had joined the parrot and dropped off to sleep. "They'll soon be waking everyone up with their silence," he thought, though he still found it very hard to believe that such a thing could happen.

John was beginning to feel very tired too, so he went on to the bedroom. Lying full stretch on the bed, he found an enormous monkey.

"What an extraordinary place to find a monkey," said John.

"What's so extraordinary about it?" asked the monkey.

"Nothing, I suppose," said John, "but what happens when someone else wants to sleep?"

"Don't be silly," answered the monkey. "Animals don't need beds. They can curl up anywhere and go to sleep."

When he had finished speaking, the monkey gave a huge yawn and, before John could answer, he was fast asleep.

So John tiptoed out of the bedroom. When he walked back across the landing, the house was in complete silence. All the birds were fast asleep and, when John looked at them, he felt dreadfully tired himself. He went quietly down the stairs and back into the sitting room. The lion was sitting up, rubbing his eyes with a paw and yawning.

"I hope I didn't wake you," said John.

"Not at all," replied the lion. "It was the silence."

"Ah," said John, nodding wisely. "I'm sorry to trouble you, Mr Lion . . ." he began.

THE JUNGLE HOUSE

The lion immediately sat up very straight and said sternly, "You should call me Your Majesty."

"I'm sorry, Your Majesty," said John. "I didn't know you were a king."

"Of course I'm a king," said the lion. "I'm the King of the Jungle House."

"Well, I'm sorry to trouble you, Your Majesty," John began again, "but the fact is that I'm feeling very tired myself now, and I was wondering whether you could find me somewhere to sleep."

Almost immediately, the lion stood up and gave the most tremendous roar. John was so frightened, he crawled behind a chair and covered his ears with his hands.

Then the door opened, and in walked the elephant.

"You called, Your Majesty," he said, bowing down very low. Then the brown bear walked in, followed by the giraffe and the monkey, and they all bowed down to the lion as well. Lastly, the parrot and all the birds flew into the room, loudly singing "God Save the King".

THE JUNGLE HOUSE

When they had finished, the lion said, "Our young visitor is feeling tired and he would like to sleep. Who can suggest a place where he might be comfortable?"

"I don't think he'd be very comfortable on the dining-room table," said the elephant.

"Or on the draining board," said the brown bear.

"Or in the bath," said the giraffe.

"Or in the . . ." said the monkey, but he stopped before he had finished the sentence. All the other animals had turned round to look at him, and then the monkey said, "I think he'd be very comfortable in the bed."

"Thank you," said John. "That is kind of you."

So they all bowed and walked out of the room backwards, so that they wouldn't turn their backs on the King of the Jungle House. John went up to the bedroom and, almost as soon as he lay down, he was fast asleep.

When he woke up, it was very, very quiet.

"The silence must have woken me," he said aloud. And he opened his eyes to find his mother laughing at him.

"Whoever heard of silence waking anyone up?" she said.

"It happens in the Jungle House," said John.

"You've been dreaming," said his mother.

"I suppose I have," said John, rather sadly.

Then he gave a big yawn, got out of bed, and went to the shelf where all his toy animals stood in a line. While he was looking at them, the most extraordinary thing happened – they all winked at him. First the toy lion winked, then the toy elephant, followed by the toy brown bear, the toy giraffe and the toy monkey. So what do you think John did? He winked back at them, of course.

Leaf Magic

by Margaret Mahy

When Michael ran home from school, he heard the wind at his heels rusting like a dog in the grass. As he ran, a thought came into his mind.

"I wish I had a dog. Running would be more fun with a dog."

The way home wound through a spinney of trees. It was autumn and the trees were like bonfires, burning arrows and fountains of gold. But Michael ran past without even seeing them.

"I wish I had a dog," he said aloud, in time to his running.

The trees heard him and rustled to each other.

"A dog with a whisking tail," Michael added.

The wind ran past him. Michael tried to whistle to it, but the wind is nobody's dog and goes only where it wants to. It threw a handful of bright and stolen leaves all over Michael and went off leaping among the trees. Michael thought for a moment that he could see its tail whisking in the grass. He brushed the leaves off his shoulders.

"An orange dog with a whisking tail," Michael went on, making up a dog out of autumn and out of the wind.

The trees rustled again as he left them behind and came out on to the road. Patter, patter, patter. Something was following him.

"It's my dog," Michael said, but he did not turn round, in case it wasn't.

Patter, patter, patter . . . At last Michael just *had* to look over his shoulder. A big

LEAF MAGIC

orange leaf was following him – too big to come from any tree that Michael knew. When he stopped, the leaf stopped too. He went on again. Patter, patter, patter went the leaf, following him.

Some men working on the roadside laughed to see a leaf following a boy. Michael grew angry with the leaf and ran faster to get away from it. The faster he ran, the faster the leaf followed him, tumbling like an autumn-tinted clown head over heels in the stones along the roadside. No matter how he tacked and dodged on the way home, he could not lose the leaf. He crawled through a hedge – but the leaf flew over it light and rustling. He jumped over a creek and the leaf jumped after him. What was worse, it jumped better than he did. He was glad to get home and shut the door behind him. The leaf could not get in.

Later that evening his mother went to draw the curtains. She laughed and said, "There's such a big autumn leaf out here on the window-sill, and it's fluttering up and down like a moth trying to get at the light. It looks as if it's alive."

"Don't let it in," said Michael quickly. "I think it's something horrible pretending to look like a leaf..."

He was glad when his mother pulled the curtains, but that night, when he lay in bed, something rustled and sighed on his own window-sill, and he knew it was the leaf.

Next day it followed him to school. As he sat at his lessons he saw it dancing like a flame out in the playground, waiting for him. When he went out to play, it bounced at his heels. Michael made up his mind to trap the leaf. He chased after it, but it wouldn't let itself be caught. It crouched and then flitted away. It teased him and tricked him. Michael felt that the leaf was enjoying itself thoroughly. Everybody laughed but Michael.

At last he decided he must be under some witch's spell.

"I'll have to go and ask Fish and Chips about it," he thought. "He'll know what to do."

Fish and Chips was an old whiskery man who lived in a cottage by the sea. He had built it himself. The walls were made of driftwood and fishbones and it was thatched with seaweed. Fish and Chips was not only whiskery but wise as well. He was almost a wizard really.

After school, instead of going home by the trees, Michael ran down on to the beach. He left a trail of footmarks behind him in the soft sand and the leaf skipped happily in and out of them. Once it rushed down to the sea to taste the salt water. Once it sailed up to where the sand ended and the grass began, but all the time it was really following Michael closely.

Fish and Chips was sitting at the door of his house. Michael went right up to him, but the leaf stayed a short distance away, playing by itself and watching them.

"Ah," said Fish and Chips, "I see you are being haunted. Do you want me to help you?"

"Yes, please," said Michael. "That leaf has been following me since yesterday."

LEAF MAGIC

"It must like you," Fish and Chips remarked.

"But I don't want it," Michael said. "Can you catch it?"

"Oh yes, I think so," Fish and Chips replied. "It seems friendly and full of curiosity. Let us hide behind the door and see if it comes after us."

They hid behind the door with the brooms, gumboots, raincoats and milk bottles all belonging to Fish and Chips. Through the crack in the door Michael could see the leaf coming closer and closer. It hesitated on the threshold of the cabin and then came in.

"Now!" said Fish and Chips, and Michael slammed the door shut while Fish and Chips jumped out and caught the leaf. Michael saw it twisting for a moment in his brown hands, as if he was holding a little fire. Then Fish and Chips opened a big box and dropped the leaf in. The lid slammed down. The big orange leaf was shut up alone in the dark.

"It won't trouble you again," Fish and

Chips told him.

"Thank you very much," Michael said politely. "How much do I owe you?"

"Whistle a sea chanty for me," Fish and Chips replied. "Whistle it into this bottle and I'll be able to use it again some time."

So Michael whistled "What Shall We Do with the Drunken Sailor" into the bottle. Then Fish and Chips corked it up quickly before the tune had time to get out. As Michael left he was writing a label for it.

Michael started off home slowly across the beach. All the time he was listening to hear the rustling of the leaf behind him. He kept looking back over his shoulder. Halfway across the beach he stopped. The beach looked empty without that bright leaf tossing behind him. He thought of it shut in that dark box in the seaweed-and-fish-bones cabin. How it would hate being boxed up. Suddenly he found he was missing the leaf. Michael took one more step and then he turned round and went back to Fish and Chips's cabin.

Fish and Chips was putting the bottle

LEAF MAGIC

up on a high shelf.

"What, more leaves already?" he asked.

"Well, not actually," Michael said in a small voice. "I just decided I wanted the old one back after all."

"Oh well," said Fish and Chips. "Often people do want them back, but they don't often get them back, not quite the same. They change, you know."

"Change?" asked Michael.

Fish and Chips opened his box. Out jumped a big orange dog with a whisking tail.

"Like that," said Fish and Chips.

The dog put its paws on Michael's chest and licked his face.

"My dog!" Michael cried. "It's my dog!"

He took its paws in his hands and they danced until the fishbones rattled.

"Thank you, thank you!" Michael called to Fish and Chips.

"Don't thank me," Fish and Chips said. "You did it all by coming back for your leaf. That's the way with magic. But just get out of my cabin before you shake the fishbones down."

Michael leapt out of the door and ran off along the beach. The dog came bounding after him and they set off home. As they ran under the trees, leaves fell over them like a shower of gold. The wind tried to join in the chase, but Michael and his dog were too fast for it. Trying to pretend it did not care, the wind made itself a bright scarf out of the fallen leaves and watched Michael and his autumn dog speed up the road, burrow through the hedge, jump the creek and come home at last. Laughing to itself, the wind leapt into a shining bush and sat there, rustling like a salamander in the heart of the fire.